Howling At The Hills...

Dante Howard

BookLeaf Publishing

India | USA | UK

Presentation by *BookLeaf Publishing*

Web: www.bookleafpub.com

E-mail: info@bookleafpub.com

ISBN: 9789363316768

First edition 2024

To Carter and Cheign,

*You are the future, the promise of new
beginnings and endless possibilities. Your
laughter and joy bring light into our lives, and
your curiosity inspires me every day.*

*This collection of poems is dedicated to you,
with the hope that you grow up to chase your
dreams fearlessly and embrace the beauty of
life's journey. May you always find wonder in
the world around you and know that you are
loved beyond measure.*

Baba Don

ACKNOWLEDGEMENT

To the friends and family who have been my pillars of support, your love and patience have given me the strength to continue writing. Your encouragement and belief in my work have been the driving force behind this new collection.

To the writers and poets whose works have lit the path before me, thank you for showing me the limitless possibilities of language and creativity. Your words have been both a challenge and an inspiration, pushing me to find my voice in this vast literary landscape.

To the artists whose creations have sparked my imagination, your ability to capture and convey emotion through various mediums has been a profound influence on my poetry. Your work reminds me that art, in all its forms, is a powerful conduit for human connection.

To the anonymous supporters and kind souls on social media who have shared their thoughts, offered encouragement, and connected with my work, your voices are heard and appreciated more than you know. Your feedback and enthusiasm have fueled my determination to keep writing.

Finally, to every reader who has taken the time to engage with my poetry, thank you for sharing this journey with me. Your presence and support make every moment of writing worthwhile.

PREFACE

Welcome back, dear reader, to another exploration of the mind and heart through the art of poetry. If you've traveled with me before, you'll recognize the spirit of spontaneity and adventure that guides my words. If this is your first journey with me, I'm delighted to have you along.

When I embarked on my initial foray into poetry, it was a leap into the unknown, driven by a simple desire to try something new. That first collection was a testament to the joy of discovery and the power of unfiltered expression. Encouraged by the heartfelt responses and the personal fulfillment I found in that process, I return now with a renewed sense of purpose and curiosity.

This new collection continues in the same vein—an unstructured, free-flowing exploration of thoughts, feelings, and observations. Each poem is a snapshot of a moment in time, a piece of my world shared with you in its most raw and honest form. There are no set themes or styles, only the authentic expressions of a poet on a journey.

Life, with all its complexity and beauty, continues to be my muse. The love and support of my wife, Indiria, and the joy and inspiration from my children, Chardanae, Asher, and Braedain, fuel my creative spirit. Through their eyes, I see the world anew each day, and through my words, I strive to capture those fleeting moments of clarity and wonder.

As you read these poems, my hope is that you find something that resonates with you, that sparks a thought or stirs an emotion. May these words entertain you, provoke reflection, and perhaps even inspire you to embark on your own creative journeys.

Thank you for joining me once more. Let's continue to embrace the adventure of poetry together.

Best regards,

Dante'

Cancel Culture

In the digital town square, voices rise,
Echoes bouncing off virtual walls,
A cacophony of judgment, sharp and swift,
Cancel culture, they call it, a modern trial.

No need for courts or judges' gavels,
The jury is the crowd, faceless and vast,
A misstep, a word out of place,
The verdict comes with a click, a share.

Once, we gathered to hear and debate,
To challenge, to learn, to contemplate,
Now, in the rush to be righteous and pure,
We forget the art of forgiveness, the power to cure.

A tweet from ten years past,
A comment made in a different light,
Resurrected, dissected, stripped of its time,
Context lost it's time to fight.

We wield our moral superiority,
As if we've never erred, never faltered,
Casting stones in a fragile glass house,
Ignoring the cracks in our own mirrored walls.

Who holds the power in this viral age?
Who decides what's irredeemable, what's sage?
The mob mentality, a beast unchained,
Feeds on outrage, leaves understanding maimed.

Yet, in this clamor, we lose sight,
Of redemption's gentle, guiding light,
That people change, evolve, and grow,
From ignorance to wisdom, they sometimes flow.

Is there room for grace in this canceling storm?
For dialogues that mend, not just reform?
In the silence after the outrage fades,
Do we find peace or just empty crusades?

Cancel culture, a mirror to our fears,
Reflects a society on shifting gears,
Let's not forget the human behind the screen,
In our quest for justice, let empathy intervene.

A Father Never Sleeps

When first he learns of a father-to-be,
His mind alights, with thoughts he cannot keep,
Thus begins the tale, a father never sleeps.

He dreams of how the future child will see,
The kind of dad that he will be,
Thus continues the tale, a father never sleeps.

The baby's cries at night, a soulful plea,
The endless nights, the hours that slowly creep,
Thus continues the tale, a father never sleeps.

For sports and school, he preps with glee,
Late nights, early morns, his schedule keeps,
Thus continues the tale, a father never sleeps.

The child grows up, but still the father's plea,
In the quiet house, his vigil he must keep,
Thus continues the tale, a father never sleeps.

Fatal Error

In the glow of the screen, with a sigh so deep,
An engineer toils, losing precious sleep,
His CAD design, a masterpiece in sight,
Yet fatal errors plague him, night after night.

With fingers poised, he crafts with care,
His mind sharp and keen, his vision rare,
But alas, the blue screen strikes with glee,
A digital gremlin in his machinery.

"Fatal error!" the message sneers,
In mocking tones that amplify his fears,
He curses the code, the silicon gods,
As his design vanishes, despite all odds.

He reboots the system, hope renewed,
Only to find his progress misconstrued,
The software laughs, with errors anew,
Each crash a dagger, each freeze a coup.

"Technology's grand!" the adverts proclaim,
Yet here he sits, frustrated and lame,
An artist shackled by bytes and bits,
His patience tested in endless fits.

He tries to save, but the file is lost,
A phantom lurking, at data's cost,
He dreams of paper, of pen's sweet grace,
A simpler time, a slower pace.

In this age of silicon-rich,
Efficiency is a fickle bitch,
A digital dance of dread and delight,
Where fatal errors reign, an endless sight.

So here's to the man, in tech's cruel embrace,
May his designs find a safer place,
And to the software, may it soon relent,
Or to the flames of frustration, be content.

Inflation

Increasing prices everywhere we see,
Necessities now luxuries, it seems to be,
Families struggle, budgets stretched thin,
Living costs soaring, where to begin?
All our savings, dwindling fast,
The hope for comfort, a thing of the past,
Income stays stagnant, while costs inflate,
Our dreams deferred, our fears innate,
No end in sight, this financial strain.

Knot on My Shoe

There once was a man with a shoe,
Whose laces were tied in a stew,
He tugged and he tried,
Till he tripped and he cried,
So he snipped them and started anew.

Gossip Folks
(Snakes in the Grass)

In shadows where the whispers crawl and creep,
Lies a creature of deceit, so sly and deep,
Its tongue flicks out with venomous grace,
A serpent's guise hides its true face.

It slithers close, with eyes that gleam,
In the dark corners, it weaves a scheme,
A hiss, a word, a tale to spin,
Drawing you close, inviting you in.

Its scales are smooth, a polished lie,
Reflecting secrets, passing by,
Coiled in rumors, it strikes with speed,
Planting doubts, feeding on greed.

In the sunlit day or moonlit night,
It waits, it watches, ready to bite,
With fangs of gossip, sharp and keen,
It pierces trust, unseen, obscene.

No rattles warn of the lurking threat,
No sound betrays the plans it's set,
But once it strikes, the wound is deep,
The poison spreads, causing hearts to weep.

Beware the serpent with human guise,
Its charm a veil, its words disguise,
For in its grip, many fall prey,
To the silent venom it spreads each day.

So heed this warning, keep it near,
A snake in the grass is ever here,
Not scaled or cold, but warm and kind,
A whispering tongue, a dangerous mind.

Survival

In a world where shadows drape the earth,
Where silence reigns and life's dearth,
We tread the ruins, memories' ghost,
Survivors' song, a silent toast.

The cities crumbled, ash and dust,
Steel and stone, now turned to rust,
A sunless sky, the world grown cold,
Survival's tale, a story told.

Once, gardens bloomed and rivers ran,
Now barren wastelands, desolate span,
The wind's harsh whisper, a mournful cry,
Of days gone by, of dreams run dry.

To live, we scavenge, piece by piece,
For food and shelter, never peace,
A simple fire, a precious light,
In the endless dark of eternal night.

Water's worth its weight in gold,
A sip, a drop, a story told,
Of struggles fierce, of battles won,
Beneath the unforgiving sun.

Community, a fragile thread,
Of trust and care in a world so dead,
We band together, hand in hand,
To reclaim hope in this broken land.

Skills forgotten, now prized once more,
To hunt, to build, to heal the sore,
Ingenuity, our saving grace,
In the harshness of this barren place.

The heart must harden, yet remain kind,
For love's the beacon we must find,
In the rubble of a world undone,
A spark of humanity, a rising sun.

Yet every night, we dream and grieve,
For what was lost, what we believe,
An elegy for a world so grand,
Now reduced to dust and sand.

Survival's creed, a hymn we sing,
Of resilience in the face of suffering,
With courage, grit, and hope's bright flame,
We strive to live, to reclaim our name.

In this post-apocalyptic strife,
We seek the essence of true life,
To rebuild, renew, and one day see,
A world reborn, and agony free.

Are Em

Rising through the ranks, a distant dream,
Equity feels like a fading gleam,
Power held by faces often the same,
Reflecting a system that's hard to tame.
Empathy lacking in the boardroom's gaze,
Stories of struggle often left in a haze,
Endless meetings, decisions so grand,
Need voices of color to truly understand.
Talents diverse, yet opportunities few,
Ambitions stifled, dreams overdue.
To see real change, we must take a stand,
Inclusion must spread across this land.
Openness to all, the start of the climb,
Necessity for progress, it's time.

More leaders of color, in positions so high,
A diverse corporate world, let's reach for the sky,
Together we thrive, our strengths combined,
Talents unleashed, unconfined.
Every voice matters, in decisions and plans,
Representation empowers, as diversity expands.
So let's build a future where everyone can stand…

Rugby

13

Rugby,
Grit and glory,
Scrumming, tackling, scoring,
Fierce hearts collide on the green field,
Passion.

The Intern

The bustling hive of a marketing firm,
An intern moves with quiet grace,
Her presence barely a whisper
Amidst the roar of corporate ambition.

She fetches coffee with practiced hands,
A dance of cream and sugar,
A routine unnoticed, yet precise.
Envelopes and memos, her daily companions,
She delivers them with silent efficiency,
A ghost in the machine.

Her voice, a hidden note in the office symphony,
Rarely heard, rarely sought,
Yet her eyes, they gleam with unspoken thoughts,
Ideas flicker behind her calm facade,
Waiting for a spark, a chance to ignite.

In the conference room, tension hums,
Brainstorms falter, creativity stalls,
The great minds gather, their efforts strained,
Frustration cloaks the air, thick and stifling.

And then, from the corner, a hesitant breath,
She speaks, a single idea, crystalline and bold,
Cutting through the haze of doubt,
A revelation, simple yet profound.

The room falls silent, eyes turn her way,
Recognition dawns, a collective awe,
Her quiet brilliance, now in full display,
She transforms, from shadow to light.

Applause erupts, a tide of admiration,
Her name, once whispered, now a chant,
In that moment, she steps into her power,
Promoted, elevated, a beacon of innovation.

No longer just an intern, a silent helper,
She claims her place among the stars,
Her journey, from shadows to spotlight,
A testament to the power of quiet strength,
To the hidden potential in us all.

Interwebs

Ode to the Internet, vast and grand,
A web of wonders at our command,
With cables and signals, you span the earth,
A digital realm, of endless worth.

From humble beginnings, you grew with grace,
Connecting hearts in a boundless space,
A tapestry woven with threads of light,
Binding the world, day and night.

In the dawn of your birth, we marveled in awe,
At the magic you brought, without flaw,
From emails to chats, your gifts were clear,
Bringing distant loved ones near.

Knowledge flows like a river, uncontained,
In your depths, wisdom is gained,
From ancient texts to modern prose,
In your embrace, our curiosity grows.

Ode to your forums, your bustling streets,
Where minds converge, and ideas meet,
A marketplace of thoughts, free and wide,
A haven where creativity resides.

Yet, within your vast and intricate weave,
Lies a dual nature, hard to perceive,
For in your shadows, dangers lurk,
Misinformation and malice, at work.

But let us not dwell on the darkened trace,
For in your expanse, there's ample grace,
You empower voices, once confined,
Giving strength to the human mind.

Ode to the Internet, connector of souls,
A bridge to our dreams, our shared goals,
In your code, we find unity's song,
A testament to a world where we all belong.

Check/Mate

The realm of myth, where legends reside,
Where kings and queens in grandeur abide,
Knights in armor, brave and bold,
Guard the kingdom, tales untold.

On fields of green, under the blue sky,
Dragons soar, with a piercing cry,
Breath of fire, scales agleam,
In the heart of battle, they reign supreme.

The king, a ruler wise and just,
In his decisions, the people trust,
With every move, his kingdom's fate,
Hangs in balance, early or late.

Beside him stands the queen, so fair,
With cunning mind and warrior's glare,
Her strategies, a dance of grace,
In every move, she claims her space.

Knights on horseback, swords held high,
Charge through the fray, beneath the sky,
Their loyalty, a shield of might,
In darkest times, they are the light.

The board is set, the pieces align,
A chess game's heart, a design divine,
Every move, a calculated risk,
In the shadows, dangers brisk.

Pawns advance, with hope anew,
In their simple steps, a future view,
A sacrifice, a valiant deed,
To pave the way, to meet the need.

Bishops glide on paths unseen,
Across the board, through spaces keen,
Their faith a guide, their aim precise,
In the game of life, they roll the dice.

Rooks, like castles, hold their ground,
With steadfast hearts, they circle 'round,
Defending realms with stony might,
In the endless quest, the endless fight.

Dragons clash in skies of gray,
Their fiery breath the price we pay,
For every move, a life is weighed,
In the dance of war, where fortunes fade.

In this allegory of the chessboard's art,
We find the echo of the human heart,
Kings and queens, in life's grand scheme,
Knights and dragons, dreams we dream.

For every move, a story told,
In battles fierce, in legends old,
We see ourselves, in every play,
In the game of life, day by day.

So heed the tale, the moves you make,
In every choice, a path you stake,
For in this world of strategy,
We find the heart of destiny.

Making The Band

The schoolyard's atage, bullied every day,
A kid endured the pain and stifled cries,
Determined to break free from fear's dark sway,
He sought the strength within, to rise, to try.

The bully's jeers a constant, cruel refrain,
The boy, now ready, faced the daunting task,
With fists clenched tight, he stepped into the fray,
Resolved to end the torment, shed the mask.

The clash was fierce, a battle to reclaim,
In every punch, a whisper of resolve,
Emerging from the fight, no longer shamed,
A newfound friendship started to evolve.

From foes to friends, a bond began to bloom,
Their past forgotten, now a team so strong,
In music's harmony, they found their room,
Together in a band where they belong.

The bully's scorn replaced with loyal trust,
A partnership where once was only strife,
In melodies, they turned their pain to dust,
Transforming discord into notes of life.

With every song, they wrote a tale anew,
A testament to courage and to heart,
The echoes of their past, now out of view,
In friendship's light, they forged a brand-new start.

The Artist

Brush strokes of passion,
Unseen, unloved, cast away—
Homeless artist's dream.

In shadows he lived,
Poverty his only friend,
Colors told his tale.

Silent death's embrace,
Trash yields treasures worth millions—
Fate's cruel twist revealed.

Love Endures

On a random Tuesday, where dreams converge,
Two souls met by fate's gentle urge,
Amidst the chaos, their hearts did align,
A love so profound, a bond so divine.

From dawn till dusk, they'd laugh and they'd play,
Cherishing moments, day after day,
In parks and cafes, their memories grew,
Two hearts as one, in a world made anew.

But fate's a fickle bitch, her plans unforeseen,
A job offer came, a change in routine,
One had to leave, to cross the wide sea,
To a distant land, where dreams were to be.

With heavy hearts and tear-filled goodbyes,
They parted ways under gray, somber skies,
Promises made, to keep love's flame bright,
Yet distance and time dimmed their light.

She worked in finance, a world of fast pace,
Climbing the ladder in a new place,
Her nights were long, her days were demanding,
Yet thoughts of him, her mind was commanding.

He stayed behind, in the city they knew,
Pursuing his art, his passion stayed true,
In galleries bright, his work found acclaim,
Yet whispers of her, his heart would still claim.

Years passed by, seasons turned,
Lessons were learned, bridges were burned,
Both found success in their separate ways,
But shadows of love haunted their days.

Then came a convention, a grand affair,
Bringing together people from everywhere,
Amidst the crowd, their eyes did meet,
A spark rekindled, a moment so sweet.

Surprised and elated, they talked for hours,
Recounting the years, their separate towers,
Laughter and tears, a reunion of souls,
Old love renewed, making them whole.

They spoke of the past, the what-ifs and why,
The paths they had taken, the reasons they'd cry,
But now in each other, they saw the truth,
A love that endured, unwavering, uncouth.

Hand in hand, they vowed to start anew,
To cherish the present, and each moment true,
For love, once lost, had found its way,
To reunite hearts, come what may.

Dark Of The Moon

On the dark side of the moon, they dwell,
In hushed silence, where secrets swell,
Aliens with eyes, wide and keen,
Gazing at Earth, lost in a dream.

From their lunar perch, they peer below,
At a world of chaos, sorrow, and woe,
Through cosmic lenses, they watch and sigh,
Puzzled by the turmoil passing by.

They see the hungry, desperate and thin,
Children's faces gaunt, hope wearing thin,
Wars raging, nations torn apart,
Violence and greed, breaking hearts.

"Why do they fight?" the aliens ponder,
In their moonlit realm, where peace is fonder,
"Why do they starve, when abundance lies,
Within their reach, beneath their skies?"

They witness the waste, the endless greed,
Resources squandered, while many plead,
For just a morsel, a chance to live,
In a world where few are willing to give.

The aliens wonder, in their lunar night,
Why humans falter, with so much in sight,
For in their world, cooperation thrives,
A unity that nurtures all their lives.

They shake their heads, with silent grace,
At the Earthly woes they can't embrace,
For in their hearts, they cannot see,
Why conflict shrouds humanity.

In lunar stillness, they hold their gaze,
Hoping one day, Earth will change its ways,
From their dark side home, they dream of peace,
A world where suffering and strife will cease.

Until that day, they watch and yearn,
For Earth's lost harmony to return,
Aliens on the moon, with eyes so wise,
Long for a day when love will rise.

Step Right Up

Step right up, come place your bets,
In this grand carnival of loss and regrets,
Where fortunes teeter on a dice's roll,
And dreams of riches swallow your soul.

Welcome to the glittering hall,
Where luck is is key, and pride will fall,
A world where hope is bought and sold,
For promises of glittering gold.

Spin the wheel, watch it go round,
In this circus, where no limits are found,
Your hard-earned cash, a fleeting delight,
Gone in the flash of a neon light.

The slot machines clink, their siren song,
Whispering secrets of right and wrong,
"Just one more pull, you'll hit the jackpot!"
While your savings dwindle, and luck's forgot.

Roulette spins with a devil's grin,
Red or black, you'll never win,
A game of chance, a dealer's grace,
That leaves you yearning for an ace.

"Double or nothing!" the bold declare,
While caution's ghost is lost in the air,
Risk it all, the thrill's so sweet,
Till reality drops you on the street.

Oh, the tales of gamblers' delight,
Of fortunes won, of victory's height,
Yet for every story of glorious gain,
A thousand more sing a sorrowful refrain.

So step right up, and join the dance,
In this grand ballet of happenstance,
But heed this rhyme, a gambler's lament,
For every dollar lost, a lifetime spent.

A satire spun from truth's cruel jest,
Gambling's allure, a treacherous quest,
In pursuit of dreams that often stray,
To lead you far from fortune's way.

Got em...

An upscale bar, where cocktails flow,
And the chatter of those in the know,
A bartender works with grace and flair,
Her presence, a magnet in the upscale air.

She mixes drinks with a practiced hand,
Serving the city's elite, the polished, the grand,
Men in suits with confident eyes,
Drawn to her charm, their futile tries.

Each night they flock, with lines and grins,
Hoping to win her heart, yet no one wins,
She smiles politely, but never sways,
Her heart a mystery, in this nightly maze.

Whispers float all through the air,
Why won't she date? It seems unfair,
Their curiosity, a quiet storm,
In the lower region where desires form.

But one fateful evening, under soft, dim light,
Her girlfriend enters, a radiant sight,
They share a kiss, tender and true,
A love revealed, in plain view.

The men watch, their questions dissolve,
In that moment, their thoughts evolve,
Respect replaces the flirty tide,
As they see the love she does not hide.

No longer pursued, she finds her peace,
Her nights of work bring quiet ease,
Her friend's embrace, a crafted guise,
A kiss to open the men's eyes.

Pretty Brown Eyes

Her eyes, a canvas, painted with grace,
Reflecting warmth in a tender embrace,
Depths of amber, rich and profound,
Where secrets and mysteries quietly abound.

In their gaze, I found a tranquil shore,
A place where sorrows could trouble no more,
Soft as the dusk, with a calming light,
Guiding the heart through the darkest night.

Every glance, a melody sweet,
A song of solace where hearts can meet,
In those pretty brown eyes, a world anew,
A realm of wonder, pure and true.

They speak of kindness, of strength untold,
Of tales of courage, both young and old,
A spark of life, a timeless fire,
In those brown eyes, I see my desire.

For in their depths, a promise lies,
Of endless love beneath endless skies,
A woman's essence, pure and wise,
Revealed within her pretty brown eyes.

The Cat

The shadows of night, where whispers lie,
There prowls a cat with an ominous eye,
Its fur as dark as midnight's deep,
And secrets in its presence never sleep.

Upon its path, misfortune trails,
A tale of woe that seldom fails,
For those who cross its silent tread,
Will soon find themselves among the dead.

Eyes that gleam like hellish fire,
It prowls and waits, with dark desire,
Each purr a portent, each meow a knell,
A silent harbinger of doom to tell.

First was the lady, kind and dear,
Who fed the cat without a fear,
Her body found, so cold and still,
A mystery no one could fulfill.

Then came the tailor, old and wise,
Who sewed by fire under winter skies,
He stroked the cat, his fate was sealed,
Next morning, lifeless, he was revealed.

Neighbors whispered, but dared not say,
That the cat brought death, night and day,
For who would believe such a tale so grim,
A creature innocent, with a fatal whim.

And I, who pen this dreadful verse,
Have seen the cat, its deadly curse,
Emerald eyes that haunt my dreams,
With silent steps and eerie schemes.

No one believes the horror I tell,
Of the cat that weaves a lethal spell,
But mark my words, and heed with care,
The killer cat is always there.

When the world's asleep, in heart of night,
The cat from shadows softly creeps,
And those who cross its cursed path,
Shall feel the sting of silent wrath.

Beware the cat with eyes aglow,
For where it treads, death's sure to follow,
A specter in the moon's cold light,
A killer cat in the dead of night.

King

Brightens every room with his joyful smile,
Radiates kindness, going the extra mile.
Amazing imagination, boundless and free,
Empathy flows, like a vast, caring sea.
Determined in spirit, never afraid to try,
Adventurous heart, aiming for the sky.
Incredibly thoughtful, wise beyond years,
Nurtures loved ones, drying their tears.